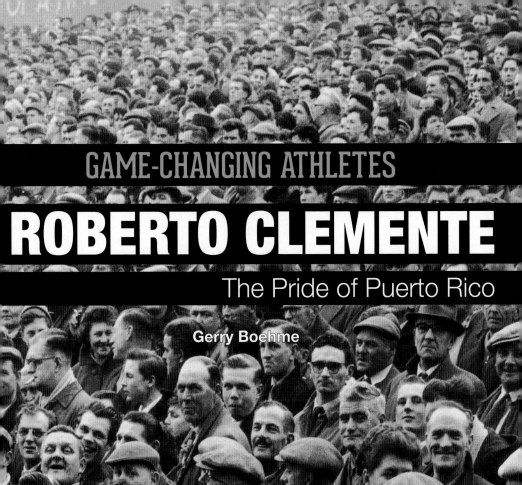

GAME-CHANGING ATHLETES

ROBERTO CLEMENTE

The Pride of Puerto Rico

Gerry Boehme

Cavendish Square

New York

Published in 2016 by Cavendish Square Publishing, LLC
243 5th Avenue, Suite 136, New York, NY 10016

Copyright © 2016 by Cavendish Square Publishing, LLC

First Edition

CPSIA Compliance Information: Batch #CW16CSQ

All websites were available and accurate when this book was sent to press.
Library of Congress Cataloging-in-Publication Data

Names: Boehme, Gerry.
Title: Roberto Clemente: the pride of Puerto Rico / Gerry Boehme.
Description: New York: Cavendish Square Publishing, 2016 | Series: Game-changing athletes | Includes index.
Identifiers: ISBN 9781502610584 (library bound) | ISBN 9781502610591 (ebook)
Subjects: LCSH: Clemente, Roberto, 1934-1972—Juvenile literature. | Baseball players—Puerto Rico—Biography—Juvenile literature.
Classification: LCC GV865.C45 2016 | DDC 796.357092—dc23

Editorial Director: David McNamara
Editor: Fletcher Doyle
Copy Editor: Rebecca Rohan
Art Director: Jeffrey Talbot
Designer: Joseph Macri
Senior Production Manager: Jennifer Ryder-Talbot
Production Editor: Renni Johnson
Photo Research: J8 Media

The photographs in this book are used by permission and through the courtesy of: Photo File/ MLB Photos via Getty Images, cover; Keystone-France/Gamma Keystone via Getty Images, cover (background); Stephen Dunn/Getty Images, 5; Stephen Dunn/Getty Images,6; Hulton Archive/Getty Images, 8; AP Photo, 13; AP Photo/File, 17; Keystone/Getty Images, 20–21; Afro American Newspapers/Gado/Getty Images, 26; Sporting News via Getty Images, 28; Sporting News/Sporting News via Getty Images, 34; J. R. Eyerman/The LIFE Picture Collection/ Getty Images, 41; AP Photo, 43; Nina Leen/The LIFE Picture Collection/Getty Images, 46; NY Daily News Archive via Getty Images, 48; Photo File/Getty Images, 52–53; Afro American Newspapers/Gado/Getty Images, 56; Andrew Burton/Getty Images, 59; William Greene/Sports Studio Photos/Getty Images, 63; Sporting News/Sporting News via Getty Images, 68; FPG/ Archive Photos/Getty Images, 70; Hulton Archive/Getty Images, 78–79; AP Photo, 82; Focus on Sport/Getty Images, 84; MONICA M. DAVEY/AFP/Getty Images, 86; Afro American Newspapers/Gado/Getty Images, 88; Francis Miller/The LIFE Picture Collection/Getty Images, 95; Diamond Images/Getty Images, 98–99; Norman Potter/Express/Getty Images, background (used throughout).

Printed in the United States of America

CONTENTS

INTRODUCTION

After inducting its newest members in the summer of 2015, the National Baseball **Hall of Fame** included only 310 people. Out of those 310, only 215 were **major league** players. Roberto Clemente Walker joined that select group in 1973, recognized as one of the greatest to ever play the game—a significant achievement, to be sure, but "Baseball Hall of Famer" paints much too limited a picture of this larger-than-life man who is still mourned and respected more than forty years after his untimely death. In truth, few athletes have ever reached the stature of Roberto Clemente. Few people have ever compressed so much life, and so many accomplishments, into just a few short years.

Roberto Clemente was indeed a great baseball player. Perhaps the best right fielder in baseball history, he was the first **Latino** baseball player to reach three thousand career **hits**. He starred in the 1971 World Series in front of more than sixty million television viewers, a record-setting audience. He collected numerous awards, batting titles, and fielding accolades.

But Clemente also lived another full life, one devoted to service. He used his talent and fame as a stepping-stone to accomplish good for all, both in his sport and in life outside of baseball. He championed his homeland, his

Superstar player Roberto Clemente spent his entire major league baseball career with the Pittsburgh Pirates.

Roberto Clemente made sure his wife Vera, three sons, and his parents Melchor and Luisa, joined him when the Pirates honored him on July 24, 1970.

race, and those in need of help. Fiercely proud, Clemente was raised to respect all people, regardless of race or wealth. He insisted that he be respected as a man, not just as a baseball player.

Called by some the "Latino Jackie Robinson," Roberto fought against those who would not treat him equally because of the color of his skin or the language that he spoke, paving the way for hundreds of Latino players who followed. Roberto Clemente died as he lived, perishing in a tragic accident as he tried to deliver relief supplies to a country stricken by an earthquake.

Writer Mike Freeman helped the Clemente family write a book about Roberto's life, *Clemente: The True Legacy of an Undying Hero*. Freeman once asked famous boxer Muhammad Ali to name the athletes Ali admired the most. Ali did not take long to mention Roberto Clemente. "I think the greatest thing you can say about a person," Ali said, "is that they gave their life for their cause. That's what Roberto Clemente did. He was a beautiful human being."

Roberto Clemente devoted his time on Earth to many things: his family, his sport, his people, his heritage, and his mission. He embodied pride, determination, and honor. He died supporting the principles that drove his life.

Roberto Clemente's name continues to live on—in baseball's record books, in the memories of the players he mentored, on the nameplates of the countless schools, ball fields and buildings christened in his honor, and in the causes and organizations that still serve those in need, the people that Roberto always held close to his heart. He was, and forever will be, the Pride of Puerto Rico.

Roberto Clemente first played professional baseball as a teenager with the Santurce Cangrejeros in Puerto Rico.

CHAPTER 1

THE BEGINNINGS OF GREATNESS

"I want to be remembered as a ballplayer
who gave all he had to give."

—Roberto Clemente, noted by Vicky Franchino
in her book *Roberto Clemente*

R oberto Clemente Walker is one of the most famous athletes to come from Puerto Rico. He was born on August 18, 1934, in Carolina, a town lying about 7 miles (11.3 kilometers) southeast of the capital city of San Juan.

The island of Puerto Rico is located in the northeastern Caribbean Sea, east of the Dominican Republic and west of both the US Virgin Islands and the British Virgin Islands. Puerto Rico is a small place, only about 100 miles long (161 km) and 35 miles (56 km) wide. Explorer Christopher Columbus discovered the island on November 19, 1493, and claimed it for Spain. Spain brought slaves from Africa to help the native tribes already living there work on its sugar plantations. The mix of native, Spanish, and African populations all contributed to Puerto Rico's rich heritage.

Spain controlled Puerto Rico until it **ceded** the island to the United States after the Spanish-American War in 1899. Puerto Rico has its own democratically elected government and is officially known as the Commonwealth

of Puerto Rico (Estado Libre Asociado de Puerto Rico), but as a United States territory it remains under the control of the US government.

Puerto Rico's historical connection with Spain and its mix of racial cultures played a large role in shaping Roberto Clemente's life and how he felt about his role in society. Roberto had dark skin and spoke Spanish, still Puerto Rico's primary language. Although he learned a bit of English in high school, he did not speak it well when he started his baseball career on the mainland. The language barrier and his color made Clemente feel isolated from his teammates and other people when he moved away from Puerto Rico to play **professional** baseball in the United States and Canada. The challenges that he faced helped transform him from a young but gifted teenager into the famous and influential person he became, a man who far transcended his role as a sports hero.

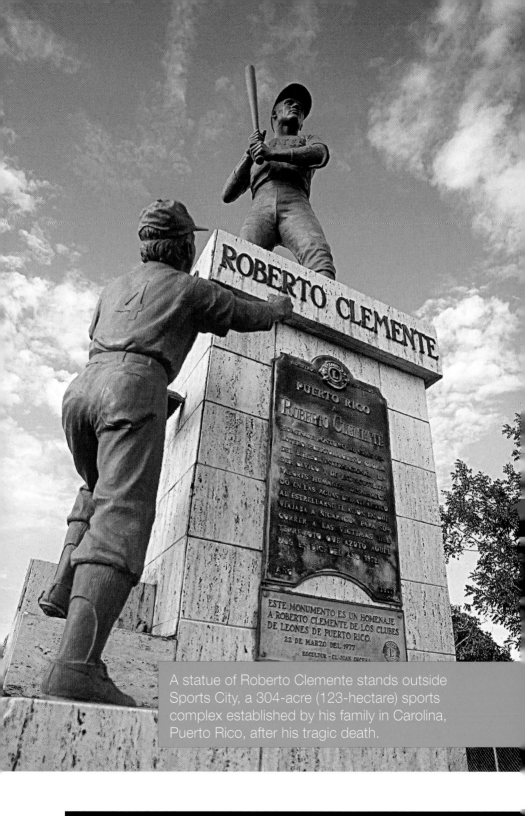

A statue of Roberto Clemente stands outside Sports City, a 304-acre (123-hectare) sports complex established by his family in Carolina, Puerto Rico, after his tragic death.

Life During a Time of Change

When Roberto Clemente was born, Carolina was a rural town that had been hit hard by the Great Depression, a period of economic hardship that also affected the United States and the rest of the world. Businesses failed and many people lost their jobs.

Clemente's ancestors had been workers on the island's coffee and sugar plantations. Roberto's father, Don Melchor Clemente, was raised during a time of great change in Puerto Rico. Slavery had been abolished on the island in 1873, not long before Melchor Clemente was born. Puerto Rico was under Spanish rule until Melchor turned fifteen.

Melchor worked at a sugarcane mill as a foreman, supervising groups of men who used machetes to cut the thick sugarcane in the fields. To make more money to support his family, Melchor also ran a small grocery store.

Roberto's mother, Dona Luisa Walker, had been married once before. After Luisa's first husband passed away, she then met and married Melchor Clemente. The family had a total of seven children, five boys and two girls, and Roberto was the youngest.

When Roberto was still an infant, his five-year-old sister Ana Iris died in a tragic household accident. Although Roberto was too young to remember Ana Iris, as he got older, he always said that he felt his sister's presence in his life.

Roberto Clemente's father Melchor worked as a foreman on a sugar cane farm similar to this one in Puerto Rico.

Melchor was already in his early fifties when Roberto was born. Roberto's father has been described as a stern and serious man who taught his children about the value of hard work, sacrifice, and the importance of helping others. Melchor wanted all of his children to carry themselves with pride and dignity. In his book *Clemente!*, author Kal Wagenheim said that Melchor told Roberto, "I want you to become a good man, a serious man."

Luisa also worked hard for her family, washing laundry for the owner of the mill and making lunches for the workers. Luisa often worked at night so that she could be home with her children during the day while Melchor worked at his job. Luisa was very religious and kind to the people in the area, often taking in and feeding poor children who came to the Clemente house.

While the Clemente family was not poor during Roberto's childhood, they had only enough money for their basic needs. They were lucky to have food, a house, electricity, and clothing, which many others did not. Roberto learned the meaning of hard work at a young age. When he was nine he asked his father for a bicycle. His father told him he needed to earn the money himself, so Roberto got up early every morning before school to deliver milk and do other jobs, saving money for three years in order to buy the bicycle.

In addition to hard work, Clemente's parents taught their children other important values, such as respect for others and the virtue of generosity. Melchor and Luisa stressed that every person was equal, regardless of the color of their skin or the amount of money they had. Roberto took that message to heart. He tried to treat everyone fairly, and he expected the same in return. Clemente fought all his life to make sure that he and other players who had dark skin and spoke a different language were treated with the same respect as white players.

Bruce Markusen, who authored a biography of Clemente entitled *Roberto Clemente: The Great One*, wrote that Roberto greatly respected his mother and father. "I owe so much to my parents," Roberto once said. "They did so much for me. I never heard my mother or father raise their voices in our home. I never heard hate in my house." Clemente loved and honored his parents throughout his life.

Roberto's parents also discouraged rash behavior, and Roberto learned to make decisions carefully. He was often quiet and shy as a child, and he usually would not do anything before thinking about it. Sometimes Roberto answered requests from his friends and teachers by saying *momentito*, a Spanish word meaning, "wait a small minute." David Maraniss, a famous writer and the author of *Clemente: The Passion and Grace of Baseball's Last Hero,* said that Clemente said "momentito" so often that his family and friends gave him a nickname, shortening "momentito" to "momen." The name stuck with Roberto for the rest of his life.

Roberto's mother strongly believed that her children should be well educated and get jobs to help people in society. During an interview with the *San Juan Star* newspaper in 1960, Luisa talked about her hopes for Roberto. She wanted him to complete school and find a career in a field like engineering rather than turn to sports. But, she said, "God wished it differently." She admitted that her son "was born to play baseball."

Little did she know that Roberto's path toward sports and stardom would have a much greater effect on people than she could ever have imagined.

Born to Play Baseball

Roberto was not a big man. Even when he reached adulthood, he was only five feet eleven inches tall (1.8 meters) and weighed 175 pounds (79 kilograms). However, he was very strong and very fast, and he had very large hands. From his early childhood, Roberto showed great athletic ability and excelled at many sports.

He often said that he inherited one of his most famous assets, his strong throwing arm, from his mother. "My mother has the same kind of an arm, even today at seventy-four," Clemente said in a 1964 interview with *The Sporting News*, a weekly magazine. "She could throw a ball from second base to home plate with something on it. I got my arm from my mother."

Clemente became a star athlete at Vizcarrondo High School in Carolina. A member of the track team, Roberto used his speed to compete in sprinting and hurdling. He also excelled at throwing the javelin, a light spear used in track events. Roberto said that throwing the javelin in high school was part of the reason he developed a strong arm. Some people believed he might be selected to represent Puerto Rico in the 1952 Summer Olympics. But from an early age, Roberto Clemente's real passion was baseball. "I wanted to be a ballplayer," he said. "I became convinced God wanted me to."

Baseball was very popular in Puerto Rico when Roberto was young. Students who returned to Puerto Rico after studying in the United States brought baseball with them, as did the US soldiers who came to the island after the end of the Spanish-American War. Many large towns and cities fielded baseball teams that competed for the island championship.

David Maraniss wrote that Roberto's older brother Justino, usually called "Matino," loved baseball as much as Roberto did. Matino was seven years older than Roberto and was the first person to really teach him the game. Roberto admired his older brother, who continued to give him advice for the rest of his life. Roberto always said that Matino was the best ballplayer in the family until he joined the US Army in 1950.

Roberto would continuously hit bottle caps with a broomstick and throw rubber and tennis balls against the walls and ceilings of his house. He made his first bat using a branch from a large tree. His fashioned his first baseball glove from a sack that was used to store coffee beans.

Nick Healy, in his biography *Roberto Clemente: Baseball Legend,* wrote that Clemente said, "I started playing baseball in the neighborhood before I was old enough to go to school. … We played until it got so dark we couldn't see. I would forget to eat because of baseball."

One day, Roberto's mother became so angry about him staying out late to play baseball that she threw his bat in the fire. Roberto managed to rescue it before it was too badly damaged.

When Roberto Clemente started playing with Matino and his other older brothers, they played softball rather than baseball. Softball is a sport similar to baseball, except that the ball is larger and a bit softer and the pitcher throws to the batter with an underhand motion. When Roberto was eight years old, he joined his first softball team with other boys from his neighborhood. It was a slow-pitch league, in which the pitcher would throw the ball slowly with a high arc towards the batter.

When Clemente was fourteen, a man named Roberto Marin saw him playing ball with friends. Marin, a part-time teacher and a salesman for a rice company, noticed Roberto's talent right away. Marin was in charge of finding players for his company softball team and he asked Clemente to play. This marked the start of a special personal relationship between Roberto Clemente and Roberto Marin, with Marin helping to guide Clemente during the early years of his long career.

Marin first placed Roberto at shortstop because he needed infield help and he wanted to take advantage of Clemente's strong arm. After a short time, however, Marin realized that Clemente's speed and arm could better be taken advantage of in the outfield. Clemente switched positions and became an outfielder, a position he would play for the rest of his life.

During this time, Clemente switched from slow-pitch to fast-pitch softball, in which the pitcher threw much harder. He adjusted to the faster speed and excelled. The other coaches and managers in the league picked Roberto to play in their "Future Stars" competition, which only included the best players in the league. Roberto was still only fourteen years old, and most of the other players were two years older.

Roberto's success in softball soon attracted notice from local **scouts** who were looking for talented players for their baseball teams. Clemente quickly moved up to a very competitive **amateur** baseball league, playing for a team owned by a man named Ferdinand Juncos.

After watching him play for nearly four years, Roberto Marin felt that the seventeen-year-old Clemente was ready to move up to professional baseball. Marin spoke to his friend Pedrin Zorrilla. Zorrilla owned the Santurce Cangrejeros, or "Crabbers," a popular professional baseball team in the Puerto Rican **Winter League**.

Many Latin American countries, including Puerto Rico, Mexico, the Dominican Republic, and Venezuela, had winter baseball leagues. In the 1950s, many experienced professional players from the United States used Winter League baseball to keep in shape during the off-season and to earn some extra money. In those days, Major League Baseball (MLB) salaries were much less than they are today.

Winter League rosters included many well-known African-American stars even before Jackie Robinson broke the **color barrier** in the major leagues in 1947 with the Brooklyn Dodgers. Many of them played in the United States in the **Negro Leagues** during the regular baseball season because of MLB's ban on players of color. Even after the color barrier was broken, black professional baseball players continued to play in Puerto Rico when their regular seasons ended.

Young players like Roberto Clemente used the Winter League to showcase their skills alongside some of the best players in the world. Author Thomas E. Van Hyning once called Puerto Rico and its Winter League "Major League Baseball's launching pad."

Roberto Marin arranged for Pedrin Zorrilla to see Clemente play, and Zorrilla was immediately impressed. Besides owning the Santurce Cangrejeros, Zorrilla also worked as a scout for an MLB team, the Brooklyn Dodgers. Zorrilla invited Roberto to a tryout camp sponsored by both the Crabbers and the Dodgers.

In those days, Alexander "Al" Campanis was the head scout for the Dodgers in the Caribbean area. Campanis knew that more than seventy young players were coming to the camp, but he had low expectations. In his experience, it was rare to find an outstanding **prospect** at an open tryout like this one. However, when Campanis saw Roberto Clemente field, hit, and throw, he changed his mind.

During one of the drills, Clemente threw a ball all the way to home plate from deep center field, a distance of about 400 feet (122 m). In his book *Roberto Clemente: The Great One*, author Bruce Markusen wrote that Campanis asked for "uno más," Spanish for "one more." Roberto's second throw was just as good. Then Clemente ran the 60-yard (55 m) dash in 6.4 seconds, less than half a second behind the world record for that distance. When he repeated that as well, Campanis knew that Clemente had the tools to be great.

A Five Tool Player

When baseball scouts evaluate players, they rate them for five particular physical skills: hitting for average, hitting for power, fielding ability, arm strength, and running speed. Scouts refer to these five skills as "tools." Great baseball players who excel at all five skills are called "five-tool players." It's hard to find players that can do all five things, and when baseball scouts find a five-tool player, they jump at the chance to recruit that player. Campanis immediately recognized Roberto Clemente as one of those rare five-tool players. Years later, Campanis told famous sportswriter Dick Young that "Clemente was the greatest natural athlete I have ever seen as an amateur **free agent.**"

Campanis wanted to sign Roberto for the Dodgers right away, but MLB required players to be at least eighteen years old to sign a **contract**. Roberto was only seventeen, so the Dodgers could not sign him after the tryout. However, Campanis decided to keep a close eye on Clemente for the future.

While the Dodgers did not sign Clemente, Pedrin Zorrilla did. The Puerto Rican League did not require players to be at least eighteen years old, so Zorrilla offered Clemente a contract to play for the Santurce Cangrejeros. The contract included a salary of $40 per week and a signing **bonus** of $500.

Willie Mays, a star baseball player for the New York Giants, played with Roberto Clemente on the Santurce Cangrejeros in the Puerto Rican Winter League.

The amount of Roberto's salary and bonus looked like a fortune to the Clemente family. It was much more money than his father or mother made for all their hard work. His parents also knew how much baseball meant to Roberto, so they agreed that he should sign with the Cangrejeros. After signing the contract with Santurce on October 9, 1952, Roberto Clemente was no longer an amateur. He was a professional baseball player.

Roberto was still in high school when he started playing in the Puerto Rican Winter League. The Cangrejeros were already a very good team, however, and they had many top African-American baseball stars in their lineup. Clemente was very excited to play with a Winter League team against major league players from the United States, but it was not easy for him to compete with older professional players at such a young age. Roberto's excitement soon turned to frustration when he found himself spending most of his time on the bench and not playing. When he did play, Roberto did not perform as well as he had hoped.

The team's manager, James Buster "Buzz" Clarkson, decided to bring Clemente along slowly, given his age and inexperience. Clarkson had been a great player in the Negro Leagues in the United States and had also played many winters in Puerto Rico. He knew what it took to be successful, and he wanted to make sure Roberto was not overwhelmed as he began his professional career.

Clarkson also tried to give Clemente advice on how to improve. For example, when Clemente was at bat he dragged his front (left) foot and would swing at almost every pitch. Clarkson told Clemente that he could be a great player but he needed to improve his footing and only swing at good pitches. Clemente took Clarkson's advice and worked hard to get better.

Although Roberto played only part-time, the Cangrejeros won the Puerto Rican championship in his **rookie** year. During his second season (1953–1954) he played alongside Willie Mays, a developing star who would hit .345 for the World Series Champion New York Giants and be named the **Most Valuable Player (MVP)** in the **National League** in 1954. He continued to get better and became a starter during the season. Playing every day and feeling more comfortable, Roberto's true skill began to emerge. Clemente finished with a **batting average** of .288 and attracted the attention of scouts from the United States.

The Brooklyn Dodgers remembered Roberto from his tryout in front of Al Campanis, but now other teams were interested in him as well. In the early 1950s, scouts from the Milwaukee Braves, New York Giants, St. Louis Cardinals, New York Yankees, and other teams came to Puerto Rico to watch Clemente play.

The Giants made the first contract offer to Clemente. While they recognized his speed and fielding ability, they weren't sure if he could hit well enough for the major leagues, so the amount they offered in the contract was not very high.

The Dodgers believed more strongly in Roberto's talent. They offered a salary of $5,000 for a year plus a $10,000 bonus. Clemente liked that the Dodgers were already famous for breaking the color line in baseball by accepting Jackie Robinson and including other black players on their team. He also was comfortable with the idea that Brooklyn was a part of New York City, a place where many Puerto Ricans and African Americans already lived. Clemente agreed to sign with the Dodgers.

The Milwaukee Braves then offered even more money, including a $30,000 bonus. Roberto did not know what to do. He did not know the Braves or the city of Milwaukee as well as he knew the Dodgers and New York. However, Milwaukee's offer was much higher.

Roberto turned to his parents for advice. Both his mother and father said that since he had already agreed to play for the Dodgers he should keep his word and go to Brooklyn. Roberto Clemente and his father signed the Dodgers contract on February 19, 1954. According to baseball writer Phil Musick, who authored *Who Was Roberto: A Biography of Roberto Clemente*, Roberto's father Melchor had to sign with an "X" since he could not read or write.

When Roberto signed with the Dodgers, scout Al Campanis pleaded with the Dodgers management to place him on the major league roster right away instead of sending him to the **minor league**s, a lower level of baseball where young players were often sent to gain experience and prepare for the majors. However, the Dodgers decided not to put Clemente on the major league roster. Instead, they assigned Roberto to their top minor league team, the Montreal Royals of the International League, where Jackie Robinson had played in 1946.

The decision to send Clemente to Montreal instead of directly to Brooklyn would play a huge role in Roberto Clemente's career. It was also a decision that the Dodgers would always regret.

When Roberto Clemente first visited the southern United States, many public services, including drinking fountains, were reserved for whites only.

CHAPTER 2

NEW LIFE, NEW CHALLENGES

"I don't believe in color. I believe in people."

—Roberto Clemente, noted by Mary Olmstead
in her book *Roberto Clemente*

When Roberto Clemente came to North America to play baseball, he experienced many things for the first time. He had to learn a new language and a new way of life. Unfortunately, he also had another new experience: racial **prejudice**. Roberto found out that some people did not like him solely because of the color of his skin.

Everything was strange and different in Montreal. Roberto was lonely, homesick, and still a teenager. The weather was much colder than in Puerto Rico. Most residents spoke French, so Clemente did not have many people to talk to. While his teammates and some Montrealers also spoke English, young Roberto had only studied English in high school and could not speak or understand it very well. This was the first time he had to really communicate in a language other than Spanish.

His new team, the Royals, played in the International League, and the league name fit. Three teams were based in Canadian cities: Montreal, Ottawa, and Toronto. The league also included a team based in Havana, Cuba, as well as four teams in the United States. Three of the US teams were located in New York State—in the cities of Buffalo, Rochester, and Syracuse. The other US team was based in Richmond, Virginia.

Victimized by Prejudice

Roberto's eyes were soon opened to something even worse than not speaking the language. When the Royals traveled to cities in the United States, and especially to Richmond, Clemente realized that people with dark skin were often treated badly.

During the late 1950s and early 1960s, most public places in the southern United States were **segregated**, meaning that blacks and whites were often separated. Some white Americans still felt that black citizens should not have equal rights. African Americans could not use hotels, restaurants, trains, busses, or even water fountains that were designated for whites only. For the first time in his life, people told Clemente that he could not eat or stay in the same places as his white teammates.

Author David Maraniss wrote: "Color of skin is noted in Puerto Rico—there is **racism** there—but it tends to be hidden and silent, with a history far different than the States." Roberto Clemente came from a place where everyone spoke his language (Spanish) and many people had dark skin like he did. He never really felt out of place until he went to play baseball in North America.

Luckily, racial prejudice was not as strong in Canada or in the cities in New York State that were part of the International League. Even so, Roberto still had trouble getting used to his new life away from home. He noticed that his teammates often separated themselves into different groups, depending on whether they were black or white. Although some of his African-American teammates had already lived this way in America, he had never experienced anything like this in Puerto Rico.

Riding the Bench

In addition to not speaking the local language and having dark skin, Clemente faced another big problem when he arrived in Montreal: he didn't play very much. He expected to take the field every day, but he often found himself on the bench instead of in the starting lineup. Even more puzzling, the manager used him more if he was not playing well, but he'd be benched if he started playing better. This odd treatment confused Roberto and made him angry. Today, more than sixty years later, baseball experts still disagree on the reasons why the Royals treated Roberto Clemente so strangely. However, at least part of the reason had to do with baseball's rules regarding new players.

At that time, Major League Baseball's rules stated that any team that paid a player more than $4,000 per year had to keep him on the major league roster. If they were not kept with the big-league club, the player could be claimed by another team in a special **draft** held at the end of the season. The major league team with the worst record chose first in the draft. The rule prevented teams with the most money from signing players and stashing them in the minors just to keep them away from other teams. Clemente's salary was above $4,000, and the Dodgers knew they could lose him in the special draft. However, the Dodgers still chose to send him to Montreal, their minor league team, instead of the major league team in Brooklyn.

Unanswered Questions

The Dodgers obviously believed in Clemente's talent and potential, so why did they risk losing him in the draft by assigning him to the Montreal Royals instead of putting him on the Dodgers? And why did they play him only part-time? Some people believe that the Dodgers knew Clemente would be a great player but thought he needed more experience. Others think that the Dodgers didn't really want him and signed him only to keep him away from their biggest rival, the New York Giants. Still others feel that the Dodgers already had enough outfielders on their team and had no room for him right then, so they tried to "hide" him from other teams by not playing him that much and only letting other teams see him when he didn't perform well. However, there may have been one more reason why the Dodgers did not add Clemente to their major league roster right away. It may have had something to do with Clemente's skin color.

The Dodgers had already made history when they brought Jackie Robinson, an African-American player, to the major leagues in 1947. By breaking the color barrier in baseball, Robinson made it easier for the Dodgers and other baseball teams to start adding black players. By the time Roberto Clemente signed with the Dodgers in 1954, several African Americans already played for Brooklyn. Some baseball historians believe that there was an unofficial agreement among the major league teams not to have more than a few black players on any team's roster. Some also think that the Dodgers management did not want more black starting players. Since Roberto Clemente had dark skin and was a Latin American, the Dodgers may not have wanted to take a white player off their team to add Clemente.

Emil "Buzzy" Bavasi was a Dodgers vice president at the time. Bavasi approved the decisions to sign Clemente to his first contract and to send him to Montreal. Years afterwards, Bavasi made contradictory statements about why Clemente played so little in Montreal. In a June 1967 issue of *Sports Illustrated,* Bavasi said that the Dodgers were indeed afraid of losing Roberto to another team in the draft. According to writer Stew Thornley, Bavasi also has said that the Dodgers' decision had nothing to do with the Giants or any agreement about race **quotas** with other teams. He did admit, however, that race did play a role in the decision. "The thought (among people in the Dodgers organization) was that too many minorities might be a problem with the white players," Bavasi said.

Brooklyn Dodgers Vice President Emil "Buzzy" Bavasi *(left)* convinced team owner Walter O'Malley *(center)* and VP of Scouting Fresco Thompson *(right)* to sign Robert Clemente to a contract.

Whatever the reason, Clemente became so unhappy that toward the end of the season he angrily left the ballpark when he was replaced during a game by another hitter. He intended to quit the Royals and return to Puerto Rico.

Carin T. Ford talked about this situation in her book *Roberto Clemente: Baseball Legend.* She wrote that Howie Haack, a scout for the Pittsburgh Pirates, had been sent to the game to see Clemente play. By chance, Haack arrived too late to see the game, so he went to Roberto's hotel to meet him. When Clemente told Haack he was going to leave Montreal and go home, Haack attempted to get him to change his mind. If he left the team, Haack said, the league would put him on the suspended list, meaning he could not play for any team and no one else could draft him.

Clemente then spoke with Al Campanis, the Dodgers scout who had seen him a few years earlier. Campanis also urged Clemente to be patient and that everything would be all right. Luckily, Clemente listened and stayed with the team for the rest of the season.

After that frustrating season with the Royals, Clemente went back to Puerto Rico to play for his Winter League team. That year the Santurce Cangrejeros boasted many star players, including Willie Mays. Roberto played left field and hit an outstanding .344, helping the team win the Caribbean World Series. Many consider the 1954–1955 Cangrejeros to be the best Caribbean baseball team of all time.

Clemente also learned a very important lesson that year. Baseball wasn't just a sport he loved to play. It was a tough and nasty business as well. All of these new experiences helped shape his outlook as he prepared to go to the major leagues.

On to Pittsburgh

Legendary baseball executive Branch Rickey moved from the Dodgers to the Pittsburgh Pirates after the 1950 season, and he knew all about Roberto Clemente's skill and promise. The Pittsburgh Pirates finished in last place that year and had the first pick in the National League baseball draft. They claimed Clemente from the Dodgers on November 22, 1954. According to Ford, when Roberto heard that he was drafted by Pittsburgh, he said, "I don't even know where Pittsburgh is."

During the off-season in Puerto Rico, tragedy again struck the Clemente family. Roberto's brother Luis became ill with a brain tumor, and Roberto often visited him in the hospital. Shortly before Luis died from his illness, Roberto was driving home from the hospital when his car was hit by a speeding drunk driver who ran a red light. He injured his back in the accident, and back pain would bother him for the rest of his life.

Roberto did not have much time to recover from the accident before he had to join his new team, the Pittsburgh Pirates, for spring training in Fort Myers, Florida. Returning to the southern United States, he once again faced the racial prejudice that he had experienced the previous year. During one game in Birmingham, Alabama, Roberto and two other teammates were not even allowed to play because the city had passed a law forbidding white and black players to participate in sporting events together.

The Majors at Last

The Pirates were not a strong team when Clemente arrived. They had finished in last place for four of the last five years. They had not finished first since 1927 and had not won a World Series in thirty years. The Pirates played their home games in Forbes Field, a stadium with an unusually large

bob clemente

Early baseball cards identified Roberto Clemente as "Bob," even though his signature showed his correct first name.

PITTSBURGH PIRATES
OUTFIELD

outfield. When Roberto saw the long distances from home plate to the outfield fences, he decided to try to hit **line drives** rather than **home runs**. Line drives don't carry into the outfield seats, but on bigger fields they can turn into **doubles** and **triples**.

Clemente played well enough in spring training to make the Pirates' major league roster, but he did not win a starting position when spring training ended. He first wore the number 13 but quickly switched to 21 when another player gave it up. According to Ford and other writers, Roberto said he chose "21" while sitting in a movie theater by counting up the total number of letters in his full name—Roberto Clemente Walker.

On April 17, 1955, Roberto Clemente had his first at-bat in the major leagues. In a twist of fate, the Pirates were playing the Brooklyn Dodgers, the team that originally had signed Roberto to a contract. He reached base in his first at-bat and scored his first major league run. He impressed his manager and stayed in the lineup, finishing his first week of regular play with nine hits.

As the season went on, however, Roberto began to struggle. Opposing pitchers saw that he was a "free-swinger," meaning that he would often swing wildly at pitches that were far from the strike zone. He also stood very far from the plate, making pitchers think they could get him out by throwing the ball on the outside part of the plate and making him chase the ball.

SCORECARD

Major League Career Statistics:

Games: 2,433, all with Pittsburgh

Seasons: 18

Batting Average: .317

Hits: 3,000

Doubles: 440

Triples: 166

Home Runs: 240

RBIs (runs batted in): 1,305

Outfield **Assists**: 266 (NL record five times leading league)

Awards:

Major League Baseball Hall of Fame, 1973; World Series MVP (Most Valuable Player), 1971; World Series champion, 1960 and 1971; All-Star Games, 12; Gold Gloves (best fielder at his position), twelve consecutive years for right field, 1961–1972; National League MVP, 1966; *Sporting News* Player of the Year, 1966; NL batting titles in 1961, 1964, 1965, and 1967; NL Player of the Month for May 1960, August 1967, and July 1969; Congressional Gold Medal, 1973; Frank Slocum Big B.A.T. Award, 2002; Presidential Medal of Freedom, 2003; Commissioner's Historic Achievement Award, 2006.

Roberto Clemente crosses home plate after hitting one of his four home runs for the Pirates in 1959, one year before his breakout season.

Clemente soon was not playing regularly, and he again became frustrated. Like many young players, he was impatient and wanted success right away. He sometimes let his temper get the best of him, and he exploded on the field or in the clubhouse. After being fined several times by the Pirates for bad behavior and for damaging team equipment, Clemente decided that he needed to act with more maturity and correct his behavior, both to improve his image and also to save money.

Feeling Out of Place

Even though Pittsburgh was not in the southern United States, Roberto Clemente still did not have an easy time living there. Just like when he was in Montreal, Clemente often felt lonely in Pittsburgh. He missed his family, his life, and Puerto Rican food, such as fried plantains (a fruit much like a banana) and rice and beans. He also missed his homeland's weather, which was usually warm and sunny compared to cold, cloudy, and rainy Pittsburgh. To make things worse, there were few Latinos or African Americans living in Pittsburgh. Clemente was both black and Hispanic, which made his life even more difficult. He was viewed as a black man because of the color of his skin, but American blacks did not easily accept him because he came from another country and spoke mostly Spanish.

Many people in Pittsburgh, even his teammates on the Pirates, made fun of the way he talked. Some Pirate players used racial slurs when talking about him. Author Herôn

Márquez wrote about Clemente's situation in his book *Roberto Clemente: Baseball's Humanitarian Hero.* While some fans loved him, Márquez wrote, others sent him letters calling him racist names and telling him to return home to the "jungle."

Problems with Reporters

When Clemente joined the Pirates, he was also surprised at the treatment he received from writers and announcers. Many people in the United States were not yet familiar with Latin American names and customs. The Census Bureau did not even track the Hispanic population until 1970. So people called him "Bobby" or "Bob" instead of "Roberto." They even thought his full name was Roberto Walker Clemente.

In truth, Clemente's real name was Roberto Clemente Walker. As they do in many Latino countries, Puerto Ricans use two last names. Roberto's first name was followed by his father's last name and then his mother's last name. Clemente was a proud man. His parents taught him to respect all people, and he felt he should be respected in turn. He also believed that he should speak up when he felt strongly about an issue. He spoke loudly and proudly of his Puerto Rican heritage and asked to be called by his true name, Roberto.

Sportswriters and announcers who covered the Pirates were not used to hearing athletes speak out so openly about things they didn't like, especially African-American and

Latino players. Clemente's outspoken nature and Puerto Rican heritage sometimes led reporters to write negative things about him. In the press, writers emphasized his origins and appearance, calling him a "dusky flyer" and a "chocolate-colored islander."

Some newspaper writers made the problem worse when they interviewed Clemente and other Latinos. Roberto could speak English but, like many people using a new and unfamiliar language, his pronunciation and grammar were far from perfect. While baseball writers often corrected the grammar of white players when they wrote stories, some writers quoted Latino players exactly, writing how the words sounded rather than what they meant.

In the biography that he wrote about Roberto Clemente, author Bruce Markusen included an article he found in *The Pittsburgh Press*. The writer quoted Clemente as saying, "I no play so gut yet. Me like hot weather, veree hot. I no run fast in cold weather." Articles like these made Clemente and other Latin players appear less intelligent than they were.

Sometimes Latin American players were also accused of being lazy or faking an injury if they missed a game because they were sick or ill. Roberto suffered many injuries during his career, and he became upset when his manager or reporters didn't believe him when he said he was hurt. Some writers called Roberto a hypochondriac, someone who says he is ill or injured when he isn't. People said at the time that white players did not complain about injuries and played through pain better than Latin American players.

Even if some writers did not let Clemente's race affect their reporting, they still misinterpreted some things that he said because they did not understand how differently he was brought up in Puerto Rico. For example, when someone said that Clemente was the best right fielder in baseball, he agreed and said he worked hard to be the best. Many journalists thought that he was bragging and conceited. However, while people in the United States were expected to be modest and say they didn't deserve the compliment, people in Puerto Rico are taught to accept compliments and agree to them. Roberto was only reacting the way that he was taught.

Sportswriter Phil Musick, who long covered Clemente's career, admitted years later that he was one of those who focused more on racist characterizations of Clemente than on his skills as a player. Musick later apologized in his 2001 book *Reflections on Roberto*, writing, "There was a racial overtone to much of what was written about Clemente early in his career, and unfortunately it precluded much reporting on his baseball skills and how they were acquired. The author of this work [Musick] bears some of that responsibility."

Some African-American players told Clemente not to say anything about how he was treated, telling him that he could not change anything and that he might make things worse. However, Clemente did not think that was right and continued to get angry when he or his teammates were mistreated due to their race and heritage. Roberto

Roberto Clemente with St. Louis Cardinals
Tim McCarver (center) and Orlando Cepeda
(right) in 1967. Clemente and the powerful
Cepeda were the first Puerto Rican MLB stars.

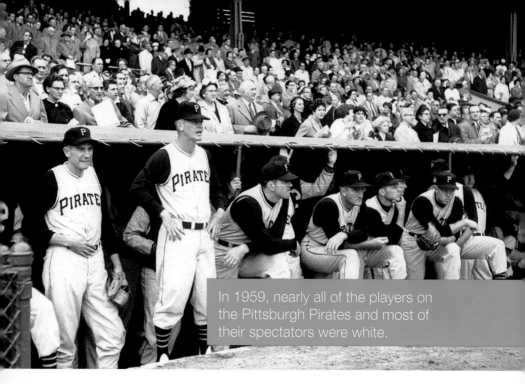

In 1959, nearly all of the players on the Pittsburgh Pirates and most of their spectators were white.

always had trouble understanding why people felt that way about him and other players of color, or those who spoke a different language.

Years later, Clemente was able to see clearly how much he had to learn as a rookie with the Pirates. "I wasn't ready for the majors when I joined the Pirates in 1955," he said, according to author Bruce Markusen. "I was too young and didn't know my way around."

After leading the team in hitting for the early part of his first season, Clemente finished with only a .255 batting average and five home runs. While the Pirates again finished in last place, Roberto did show the first signs of how popular he would become with the Pittsburgh fans. He would sign autographs long after the game ended, and some fans would even bring him sandwiches to eat between the first and second games of **doubleheaders.**

Signs of Things to Come

When Roberto returned to Pittsburgh for the start of his second season, the team had made many changes. In addition to hiring a different manager and adding some new players, the Pirates also asked former baseball star George Sisler to help Clemente with his hitting. A great hitter, Sisler had already been elected to the baseball Hall of Fame. He worked with Clemente on his batting style, and it worked. After two months of the season, Clemente was third in the National League in batting average, which is the percentage of hits per times at bat not counting walks or sacrifices. He finished the season hitting .311. Any batting average higher than .300 is considered to be outstanding, so Clemente was proving to be a star player.

Clemente also impressed people with his fielding skill and his powerful throwing arm. According to writer Vicky Franchino, famous broadcaster Vin Scully once said, "Clemente could field a ball in Pennsylvania and throw out a runner in New York."

After the season, Clemente received a raise in pay from the Pirates and used some of that money to buy his parents a new house. Kal Wagenheim wrote that Clemente said, "I am trying to pay my parents back for giving me so much."

Roberto was starting to show what he could do. In just a couple of years, he'd perform on the World Series stage for the first time.

Roberto Clemente displays his legendary throwing ability in Yankee Stadium during the 1960 World Series.

CHAPTER 3

STARRING ON THE NATIONAL STAGE

"Just the best player in baseball, that's all."

—Pirates manager Harry Walker,
talking about Roberto Clemente

After the 1958 baseball season, Roberto Clemente served in the Marines for six months. The training and physical exercise that he went through during boot camp seemed to improve Clemente's back. He had another good year after returning to the Pirates from the Marines, but the team finished only in fourth place in 1959.

Clemente and the Pirates finally put it all together in 1960. He had his best season so far, hitting .314 with 94 **runs batted in** (RBIs). The Pirates finished first in the National League and went on to face the **American League** Champion New York Yankees for the major league baseball championship. The Pirates had not played in the World Series in thirty-five years. Whichever team won four games would win the series. After six games were played, the Pirates and the Yankees were tied with three wins apiece. It would all come down to the seventh game, to be played at Forbes Field in Pittsburgh.

In a tense, back-and-forth matchup, each team took turns taking the lead and then falling behind. The Yankees were winning, 7 to 4, in the bottom of the eighth inning when the Pirates came back with five runs to take a 9 to 7 lead. Roberto Clemente kept the rally alive when he beat out a ground ball to first base, outrunning the first baseman of the Yankees to the bag and extending the inning.

The Yankees tied the game in the top of the ninth by scoring two runs. Then, with the game tied in the bottom of the ninth, Pirates second baseman Bill Mazeroski led off and hammered a home run over the left-field wall. The Pirates had finally won the World Series and become champions. Clemente batted .310 in the World Series and had at least one base hit in all seven games. He also had the most hits (nine) of any Pirate.

It would take another eleven years for the Pirates to return to the pinnacle of Major League Baseball and win another World Series. It would also take that long for Roberto Clemente to finally be recognized as one of the greatest baseball players to have ever played the game.

Disappointment, then Determination

After the season, Roberto Clemente's teammate, shortstop Dick Groat, won the league's MVP award. Groat hit .325 that season but only had two home runs and fifty runs batted in. Clemente had hit .314 with ninety-four runs

Pirates second baseman Bill Mazeroski set off a wild celebration when he homered in the bottom of the ninth inning in game seven to win the 1960 World Series.

batted in and sixteen homers. Even though his performance was better than Groat's in most areas, Clemente only finished eighth in the voting for MVP. According to Bruce Markusen, Roberto thought he deserved to finish higher in the vote and was so angry that he refused to wear his World Series ring.

Bitter about not being more strongly considered for the league MVP award, Clemente was determined to prove his ability the next season. He started strongly and was chosen to play right field for the National League in the **All-Star Game** that July. Roberto won the All-Star Game with a hit in extra innings—if a baseball game is tied after the regulation nine innings, the teams play until one team is ahead at the end of a full inning—and continued his hot hitting for the rest of the year, ending the season with the highest batting average (.351) in the National League. Clemente was the first native Puerto Rican to win the National League batting title.

According to author Carin T. Ford, the batting title meant the world to Clemente. Not only did Roberto Clemente set out to be the best ballplayer in the league in 1961, she wrote, but he also felt pride in his accomplishments as a Puerto Rican. His fellow countrymen were equally proud. Like many Puerto Ricans, Clemente had loved baseball from the time he was young. Back then, Babe Ruth was considered the best player of all. "But Babe Ruth was an American player," said Clemente. "What we needed was a Puerto Rican player they could say that about, someone to look up to and try to equal."

Clemente Credits Clarkson

Clemente credited his manager in Santurce, Buzz Clarkson, with helping him as he started his professional career. Clemente was just out of high school, and he was playing against grown professionals who often shunned first-year players. This treatment could make young players feel worthless. Clarkson said his main job was to keep up the spirits of his teenage player.

In an interview for the *Sporting News*, Clemente said, "I played for his team, and I was just a kid. He insisted the other players allow me to take batting practice, and he helped me."

Clemente also said that Clarkson fixed a flaw in his form that hurt him when he batted. The player would drag his left or front foot back and toward the third-base dugout when he swung the bat. This pulls the hitter's momentum away from the ball, reducing power. Clarkson put a bat behind Clemente's left foot so that he would step on it if he moved the foot in the wrong direction. The young player began striding properly toward the pitcher, and his results improved.

Clemente told writer Ira Miller, "The fellow who helped me most of all is [Buster] Clarkson. Buzz Clarkson used to tell me I am as good as anyone in the major leagues. That helped me a lot." Clemente would never forget Clarkson's help, and even when he became a star with the Pirates, he would speak highly of Clarkson to anyone who would listen.

Included in the Clemente family's book about Roberto is an interview with Clarkson conducted just before Clemente's death. Clarkson said, "I could see he was going a long way. ... He had a few rough spots, but he never made the same mistake twice. I told him he'd be as good as Willie Mays someday. And he was."

Another Puerto Rican player, Orlando Cepeda of the Giants, led the league that year in home runs and runs batted in. Roberto Clemente and Orlando Cepeda had combined to give Puerto Ricans the National League Triple Crown, a term given to the person who wins baseball's top three batting categories—batting average, home runs, and runs batted in. While the actual Triple Crown award can only be given to one player who wins all three categories, Puerto Ricans were happy to say that their countrymen teamed up to win this famous award.

Clemente finished fourth in the National League MVP voting that year, but his greatest reward was the reception that he and Orlando Cepeda received when they traveled home together to Puerto Rico. More than eighteen thousand fans met them at the airport, and another five thousand crowded into the local baseball stadium to greet them there.

Once again Clemente played in Puerto Rico's Winter League. Over the years the Winter League had become less popular with Major League players. Their salaries had increased and they no longer needed to earn extra money after their regular season ended in the States. Roberto, however, thought that continuing to play in the Winter League was a good way for him to thank the Puerto Rican people for their support.

Love, a Wife, and a Family

When he returned to Puerto Rico after the 1963 season, Clemente met Vera Christina Zabala in a drugstore. Vera

Roberto Clemente; his wife, Vera; and their three sons (Roberto, Jr.; Luis; and Ricky) on "Roberto Clemente Night" in New York.

was twenty-three, and the twenty-nine-year-old Roberto fell in love at first sight. Vera later told Steve Wulf of *Sports Illustrated* magazine that, "On our first real date, he told me he was going to marry me. On our second date he brought pictures of houses."

On their first date, they went to a baseball stadium in San Juan. Vera did not know much about baseball and also was not aware that Clemente was a professional baseball player. She soon found out how famous he was, as people would surround them when they went out in public.

Roberto and Vera married on November 14, 1964. They bought a house in a wealthy section of Rio Piedras. Over the years they started a family and had three children— Roberto Jr., Luis, and Enrique (Ricky). Because Roberto Clemente always took such pride in his Puerto Rican heritage, he thought it was important for his children to be born in his native land. Vera agreed. During the 1965 season, when Vera was ready to give birth to their first child, she flew back to Puerto Rico, and Roberto Jr. was born there in August. The couple also made sure that Vera was in Puerto Rico when Luis and Ricky were born.

Before the start of the 1965 season, Clemente badly injured his leg while mowing his lawn in Puerto Rico. While recovering from his injury he also caught **malaria**, which sent him back to the hospital. Roberto lost weight and reported to the Pirates for spring training late and in a weakened condition.

He got stronger as the year went on, however, and had one of the highest batting averages when the All-Star team was chosen. Although he was picked as a reserve, Clemente was upset that he was not elected as the starting All-Star right fielder. At first, he threatened not to play in the game, but cooler heads prevailed. He played after the new Pirates manager Harry Walker convinced him it would be a bad idea not to go.

When the season ended, Clemente had won his third National League batting title with a .329 average, placing him in the company of Hall-of-Fame players such as Rogers Hornsby, Stan Musial, Honus Wagner, and Paul Waner.

Becoming a Mentor

During the 1966 season, Roberto Clemente had his first real chance to become more than a star player for his team. In 1958, the Giants had moved from New York to San

Roberto Clemente mentored outfielders Matty Alou *(left)* and Manny Mota *(right)* when they joined the Pirates.

Francisco. Matty Alou, an outfielder for the Giants for six years, was traded to the Pirates in 1966. Matty Alou was not a powerful player, yet he always took a big swing and tried to hit the ball towards first base and right field. That is called "pulling the ball," since Alou was a left-handed hitter and stood on the first-base side of home plate. Walker felt that Alou could be a more effective hitter if he hit the ball harder to all fields.

Matty Alou had been born and raised in the Dominican Republic. When Alou came to the Pirates, he spoke Spanish but little English and was hitting only .230. Walker asked Roberto to help make Alou feel more comfortable. Walker also wanted Clemente to teach Alou how to control his bat better and hit the ball to all fields. Roberto appreciated that Walker respected him enough to ask his help, and he eagerly agreed. He worked with Alou all during spring training, standing by third base and telling Alou to try to hit the ball to him. Working with Clemente, Alou learned to hit that way, and his batting average began to climb. That year, Matty Alou had his best season, hitting .342. Alou eventually hit .300 or better in seven seasons.

Winning the MVP

Harry Walker also asked Clemente to do something else for the team that season. He challenged Roberto to hit with more power and drive in even more runs than before. Clemente delivered, reaching 29 home runs and 119 runs batted in, while also finishing fourth in the league with a .317 batting average. His overall performance was the best of his career, and baseball's writers rewarded him by finally electing him as the league's MVP. In a poll taken by the *Sporting News*, the players also picked Clemente as the National League Player of the Year. According to Ford, Pirates manager Harry Walker said, "He won the MVP because he did so many little things. He did the things that many stars don't, hustling on routine ground balls, breaking up double plays, taking the extra base."

Winning both the National League MVP and Player of the Year awards in 1966 seemed to have a strong and positive effect on Clemente. Teammates remarked that he seemed to be calmer the next year, showing less anger and

Roberto Clemente receives his second consecutive silver bat award for leading the National League in hitting in 1965 from National League president Warren Giles.

frustration than when he was younger. He may have felt that winning the awards, and his manager's respect, finally proved to everyone that he was truly a superstar. Roberto became much more comfortable using his experience and personality to help mentor younger players.

After the season, the Pirates offered a new contract to Clemente that, for the first time, included a salary of more than $100,000. While today's players make much more money, back in 1967, Clemente was one of only a few players with such a high salary. He soon proved that he was worth every penny. While the Pirates did not finish well in 1967, Clemente had another strong year. Along with 23 home runs and 110 runs batted in, he led the league with his best batting average so far, hitting .357. *Sport* magazine asked all of baseball's general managers to name the best player in baseball. They chose Roberto.

A Night to Remember

In 1970, the Pirates moved from Forbes Field to a new ballpark, Three Rivers Stadium, named for its location where the Allegheny and Monongahela Rivers meet to form the Ohio River. On July 24, a ceremony was held at the stadium to honor their great right fielder. On "Roberto Clemente Night," his family and many friends from Puerto Rico came to celebrate his accomplishments.

Clemente felt very proud to have a night dedicated in his honor. Bruce Markusen reported that Clemente told the crowd, "There are things in life that mean the most to me, my family—and the fans in Pittsburgh and Puerto Rico." Among the many gifts presented to Roberto was a check for $5,000 made out to the Children's Hospital of Pittsburgh. He liked to visit the children at the hospital during his free time, and he had asked the fans of Pittsburgh to donate to the hospital in his name. He also received a scroll that listed the signatures of more than three hundred thousand people, all collected from his homeland of Puerto Rico.

Clemente led the Pirates to a first-place finish in 1970 with his second-highest batting average ever (.352). Baseball had formed two divisions in each league the previous year, and the Pirates would have to play the Cincinnati Reds, who had finished in first place in the other division of the National League. The format for the National League Championship Series was best of five, meaning that the first team to win three games would move on to the World Series while the other team would head home for the off-season. The Pirates lost three straight close games in the **playoffs** to the Reds, falling just short of returning to the World Series.

1971 and Glory

When the 1971 season began, no one suspected that everything Roberto Clemente had accomplished was just a prelude to his greatest moment of triumph, one that would be witnessed by the entire world.

At the start of the season, Clemente was thirty-six years old. Pirates manager Danny Murtaugh wanted to make sure that his aging superstar remained healthy for the entire season, so he carefully managed his playing time and gave him days off whenever he could.

On September 1, Clemente became a part of history when all nine Pirates players who started the game were either African American or Latino. For the first time in major league history, every player in a baseball team's starting lineup was a person of color. Later that same month, more than forty-four thousand people gathered at Shea Stadium, the home ballpark of the New York Mets, to honor Clemente, a player for the opposing team.

Clemente had another great season and again helped the Pirates to finish first in their division and move on to the National League Championship Series. The Pirates would have to win three games against the San Francisco Giants in order to go to the World Series. The Pirates lost the first contest 5 to 4 but were winning the second when Roberto Clemente saved the game with a spectacular play. The Giants were trailing by two runs, but they had the bases loaded in the sixth inning with superstar Willie Mays coming up to hit. Out in right field, Clemente moved a few steps toward center field. When Mays then smacked a hard line drive to right-center field, Clemente managed to move to the ball and catch it on the fly. He could not have made the play if he had not moved toward center just before the pitch. The Pirates went on to win the game and tie the playoff series 1 to 1.

The Pirates also won the third game to get within one victory of moving on to the World Series. In game four, the Pirates fell behind by a score of 5 to 2 before coming back to tie the game at 5 to 5. Clemente had already driven in three runs when he came up to bat in the sixth inning. He hit a single to drive in the lead run then scored on Al Oliver's three-run homer. Clemente's fourth RBI stood up as the game-winner, and the Pirates moved on to face the American League champions, the Baltimore Orioles, for the world championship.

The 1971 World Series would be different than any previous championship. Before that year, every World Series game had been played during the day. For this series, baseball's owners decided to play one of the games at night for the first time. They hoped that a night game, in prime time, would attract more viewers to its television broadcasts.

The Baltimore Orioles were a powerful opponent. For three years in a row, the Orioles had won at least one hundred games and taken the American League **pennant**. The first two games of the best-of-seven World Series would be played in Baltimore. The next three would be held in Pittsburgh. If necessary, the sixth and seventh games would be played back in Baltimore.

The Orioles won the first game 5 to 3. The Pirates got only three hits, and Clemente had two of the three. The Orioles also won the second game 11 to 3. Again, Clemente was the only Pirate with more than one hit. The Pirates were two games down and in trouble as the Series headed to Pittsburgh for games three, four, and five.

The Pirates rebounded on their home field by winning game three by a score of 5 to 1. Clemente helped get things rolling by driving in a run in the first inning.

Game four was the first night game in World Series history. More than fifty-one thousand fans packed Three Rivers Stadium, and more than sixty-one million watched the game on television. It was by far the largest audience to ever watch a baseball game. Clemente starred under the lights, stroking three hits in four at-bats as the Pirates beat the Orioles by one run, tying the Series at two games apiece. More than half of the television sets in the entire country had tuned in to watch Roberto Clemente lead the Pirates in their victory over the Orioles.

Clemente had proved his stardom, in prime time, in front of millions of people around the nation. After the game, sportswriter Dick Young wrote, "The best ballplayer in the World Series, maybe in the whole world, is Roberto Clemente. And as far as I'm concerned, they can give him the automobile [the award for the outstanding player in the Series] right now." This was saying something, because the Orioles had three future Hall-of-Famers on their roster, and one of Clemente's teammates, Willie Stargell, would also be inducted into the shrine in Cooperstown.

The Pirates followed their two wins in Pittsburgh with a third, defeating the Orioles in game five 4 to 0. The Pirates were now one game away from clinching the World Series as they headed back to Baltimore. Not so fast! The Orioles knotted the Series at three games each when they

Roberto Clemente slides safely into third base during the 1971 World Series against the Baltimore Orioles. Roberto's spectacular performance made him a national star.

won game six in extra innings, 3 to 2, even though Roberto Clemente hit a home run in the third inning after hitting a triple in the first. The World Series Championship for the 1971 season would be decided by one final game.

Game seven was scoreless when Roberto Clemente came to bat against Orioles pitcher Mike Cuellar in the top of the fourth inning. Up to that point, eleven Pirates hitters failed to reach base against Cuellar. With one dramatic swing, Clemente broke the scoreless tie when he hit a long home run to left-center field, putting the Pirates ahead 1 to 0. Once again, he rose to the challenge and claimed the moment.

The Pirates later pushed across another run to go ahead 2 to 0. The Orioles managed to score in the eighth inning to cut the lead to one run, but the Pirates held on to win the last and deciding game 2 to 1. The Pirates were World Series Champions for the second time in Clemente's career. He had starred in a remarkable Series. He hit .414 over the seven games, getting twelve hits in twenty-nine at bats. He had a hit in all seven games. Two of his hits were home runs, and he drove in four runs. His tremendous performance earned him the series' MVP award.

According to writer Jon Patrick, when Clemente was interviewed in the locker room after the game, he said "Before I say anything in English, I'd like to say something in Spanish to my mother and father in Puerto Rico … *En el día más grande de mi vida, para los nenes la benedición mia y que mis padres me echen la benedición* (In the most

After leading the Pirates to victory during the 1971 World Series, Roberto Clemente won a new car for being chosen as the Most Valuable Player in the Series.

important day of my life, I give blessings to my boys and ask that my parents give their blessing)." At this time of great personal triumph, Roberto Clemente still thought to honor his parents, and Latinos everywhere, by speaking in their native language on national television.

A National Star

The 1971 World Series finally put Roberto Clemente in the nation's spotlight. He had been an outstanding player for many years, but many people around the country had not known how good he was until he proved it on the biggest stage.

Clemente was not a big-time home run hitter, so he did not receive as much attention as sluggers like Willie

Mays, Hank Aaron, and Mickey Mantle. Pittsburgh was not a major city, so the Pirates did not get as much national attention as teams like the New York Yankees or the Los Angeles Dodgers. Even more importantly, at that time there were no national sports networks like ESPN, or regional cable channels, to show baseball games at all hours and to feature great players like Clemente across the country. Most television stations and newspapers only covered their own local teams, so people outside of Pittsburgh did not have much of an opportunity to see Roberto Clemente play. David Maraniss wrote that, when a visiting writer asked a Pittsburgh man whether Clemente had ever run and thrown and hit like this before, the man responded "Yes, every day," but the out-of-town sportswriters had not seen him play every day until the 1971 World Series.

Roger Angell was one of the most famous sports reporters of the time, writing primarily for the *New Yorker*. Angell described Roberto Clemente's World Series performance in this way: "Clemente played a kind of baseball that none of us had ever seen before—throwing and running and hitting at something close to the level of absolute perfection." People began to call Clemente "El Grande," Spanish for "The Great One."

Willie Stargell hit forty-eight home runs for the Pirates that year. In his book *Roberto Clemente: Baseball Player*, author Jerry Roberts says that Clemente told Stargell, "If you guys get me to the World Series, I'll win it." Stargell said that, "It was almost like, 'You guys, sit down. I've got a job to do. I'll show you how it's done.'"

Clemente garnered respect from his opponents as well. Roberts describes how Hall of Famer Frank Robinson, who played right field for the Baltimore Orioles in the 1971 World Series, later said, "He didn't just play right field. He performed out there—whirl and throw to third base, not turn and throw, like most of us. He would whirl like a ballet dancer. Even though you were playing against him, you started to watch to see what he would do next. 'Did you see that? Did that happen? Did he really do that?' and you'd say, 'Yes, he did.' Wow!"

Clemente was greeted as a hero when he returned to Puerto Rico after the 1971 World Series. The Catholic University of Puerto Rico awarded Clemente an honorary doctorate in education, the first time they had given such an award to an athlete.

Vera Clemente waits on the beach near San Juan, Puerto Rico, for news about her missing husband, Roberto, whose plane crashed into the ocean just offshore on December 31, 1972.

CHAPTER 4

TRIUMPH AND TRAGEDY

"Any time you have an opportunity to make a difference in this world and you don't, then you are wasting your time on Earth."

—Roberto Clemente

After his triumph in the 1971 World Series, Roberto Clemente still had one goal he desperately wanted to reach. When spring training began the following year, Clemente returned to the United States determined to reach 3,000 hits. Only ten players in major league baseball history had ever achieved that total. Clemente wanted to add his name to that list. He was thirty-seven years old and no longer playing every game when he started the season needing 118 hits to reach his goal. Late in the season, Clemente got his 2,999th hit in a game in Philadelphia. Pirates manager Bill Virdon then removed him from the game so he could reach the 3,000-hit milestone in Pittsburgh, in front of his home fans.

In late September 1972, Clemente faced the great New York Mets pitcher Tom Seaver at Three Rivers Stadium. In the first inning, he hit a weak grounder that bounced over Seaver's head. Mets second baseman Ken Boswell ran in to field the ball, but it glanced off his glove and Clemente reached first base safely. The fans screamed as the scoreboard celebrated his 3,000th hit. However, the game's official scorekeeper quickly changed the mood in the stadium. He ruled that Boswell should have made the play and changed the call to an **error**. Clemente's hit total returned to 2,999, and he had to try again. Unfortunately, he failed to get any hits in his remaining at-bats as the Pirates lost the game 1 to 0. Clemente and his fans would have to wait at least one more night for the magical moment they were hoping for.

After the game, Clemente was upset that his grounder was ruled an error. When he thought about it more, he realized that he wanted a more impressive hit than a weak ground ball to reach 3,000. On September 30, 1972, the next night, he got what he wanted against Mets left-hander Jon Matlack. Clemente struck out in his first at-bat, but in the fourth inning he smashed a Matlack curveball off the left field wall for a double. The umpires stopped the game and handed Clemente the ball while the crowd celebrated. Roberto Clemente had just become only the eleventh player, and the first Latino, to reach 3,000 hits. When the inning was over, Roberto walked slowly out to his position in right field, where he acknowledged the still-roaring fans with a wave of his cap. Clemente basked in the glow of the moment. As it turned out, that double would be the last regular season hit of Roberto Clemente's career.

Virdon decided to rest Clemente for the last three games of the regular season, as the team had already clinched the division and again would face the Cincinnati Reds in the playoffs. However, the team then realized that Roberto needed to appear in only one more game to break Hall of Famer Honus Wagner's record for most career games played for the Pirates. Virdon sent Clemente out to right field for one inning on October 3 to break the record and set one more milestone as one of the greatest players in Pittsburgh's then eighty-four-year history.

The Pirates lost to the Reds in the playoffs in heartbreaking fashion—they lost the last two games of the five-game series, with the Reds scoring the decisive run in the ninth inning on a wild pitch—and their season ended. As the players prepared to return to their homes for the off-season, no one could have predicted the tragedy that would end Clemente's life just three months later.

When Clemente returned to Puerto Rico in the fall of 1972, he decided not to play winter baseball in order to rest his body. Instead, he kept busy by doing what he loved best—working with children through sports. He ran several baseball clinics for thousands of young Puerto Ricans. He also managed a Puerto Rican baseball team that went to play in the Amateur Baseball World Series in the country of Nicaragua. The trip to Nicaragua proved to be a life-changing event, not only for Roberto Clemente but for baseball, for Puerto Rico, and for the world. When Clemente went to Nicaragua for the Amateur World Series, he spent nearly a month in the country. He met many people and made many friends. Soon after he returned to Puerto Rico, on December 23, 1972, a major earthquake rocked Managua, the capital city of Nicaragua. The quake killed more than ten thousand people and left more than a quarter of a million people homeless. The damage was so extensive that Managua, the largest city in the country, had no running water or electric power.

Having just returned from the country after making many new friends, Clemente felt that he needed to do something to help the people there. He took charge of a committee to collect supplies for the victims of the earthquake. He appeared on Puerto Rican television and radio stations to ask Puerto Ricans to donate money, food, clothing, medicine, and other supplies to the effort, raising more than $150,000. He also made arrangements for ships and planes to deliver the supplies to Nicaragua. As money and goods flowed into Nicaragua from Puerto Rico and other countries, stories began to emerge that the shipments were not getting through to the people who needed help. Reports from the country said that Nicaragua's government and army were stealing the supplies and either keeping them for themselves or selling them for profit. The news angered many, including Clemente. He thought that if he went to Nicaragua to deliver the supplies personally, his fame might help get the supplies past anyone trying to block them from going to those needing help. He decided to get on the next plane to Nicaragua with a new shipment of supplies.

The airplane that was scheduled to transport the supplies was an old, four-engine model called a DC-7. The plane had previously experienced mechanical problems and some people felt it was not safe to use. The crew may also not have been qualified to prepare or fly a plane of that type. Given the danger of the flight and the conditions in Nicaragua at the time, many people urged Clemente not to go. His oldest son, Roberto Jr., even told his father that he had a dream that the plane would crash and begged his father not to take off with it. However, Clemente felt he needed to be there in person to make sure the supplies got through to the people. Focused only on getting aid to Nicaragua as quickly as possible, he ignored any doubts and made the fateful decision to board the plane along with four other men.

When the plane first tried to leave, it experienced engine trouble and had to return to the hangar. It was also dangerously overloaded, so it probably was too heavy to fly safely. On December 31, 1972, New Year's Eve, the old cargo plane finally took off from San Juan airport at about 9:20 p.m. As soon as the plane left the runway, it appeared to have problems. Some people say they heard an explosion or saw flames coming from one of the engines. Witnesses reported that the plane turned sharply left to try to return to the airport. There were several more explosions, and the plane crashed into the ocean, only one-half mile (0.8 km) from the island. On New Year's Day, January 1, 1973, friends, teammates, and fans all over the world awoke to the tragic news. People immediately began rescue attempts, which continued for eleven days. Many people came to help.

At first, the rescuers hoped to find the passengers alive. Later, they were just trying to find their bodies. Even Manny Sanguillen, a catcher with the Pirates and Roberto's close friend, joined a team of divers to search for the bodies. Only one body was ever recovered, that of the pilot, Jerry Hill. All that they ever found of Roberto Clemente was his briefcase. He was only thirty-eight years old when he died.

In his 1974 biography *Who Was Roberto?: A Biography of Roberto Clemente*, writer Phil Musick described the reaction to Clemente's death. "A resolution was introduced in the lower house of the legislature to rename the San Juan airport in honor of Clemente. A memorial fund was established to build Ciudad Deportiva [Sports City]. Children from a Brooklyn grade school pasted pennies to a sheet to form Clemente's number 21; the Pirates and a Pittsburgh foundation each donated a hundred thousand dollars to the Clemente fund. In a week the fund swelled to half a million dollars … the *Washington Post* editorialized: 'In Pittsburgh, at the empty Three Rivers Stadium yesterday, the scoreboard bore the legend, "Roberto Clemente, 1934–1972." It might have also read, "A man of honor played baseball here."

The *New York Times* reported on January 2, 1973, that Puerto Rico shut down for three days of national mourning for Roberto Clemente. Radio stations replaced their regular programs with quiet music. A memorial service was held on January 4 at the San Fernando Catholic Church

Pirates teammate Willie Stargell and his wife Margaret leave the San Fernando Catholic Church in Carolina, Puerto Rico, after a memorial service for Roberto Clemente on January 4, 1973.

Vera Clemente, widow of baseball star Roberto Clemente, wipes her eyes after accepting the Baseball Hall of Fame plaque in his honor in Cooperstown, New York, on August 6, 1973. Also inducted were pitcher Warren Spahn (*left*), outfielder Monte Irvin (*second from right*), and George Kelly (*right*).

in Clemente's hometown of Carolina. Many Pirates flew in to attend the ceremony, including three of Clemente's past managers—Danny Murtaugh, Bill Virdon, and Harry Walker. A church in Pittsburgh held a memorial Mass at the same time as the service in Carolina was taking place so that Roberto's family, friends, and fans could honor him together. A sign in Pittsburgh that usually showed advertisements was changed so that it read *Adios Amigo*, which means "Good-bye Friend" in Spanish.

According to the *Pittsburgh Press*, Baseball Commissioner Bowie Kuhn said, "Words seem futile in the face of this tragedy. Nor can they possibly do justice to this unique man. Somehow, Roberto transcended superstardom. His marvelous playing skills rank him among the truly elite. And what a wonderfully good man he was! Always concerned about others. He had about him the touch of royalty."

Soon after Roberto Clemente perished, people around the world began to offer additional tributes in his memory. Funds were raised to build a pediatrics wing at the Masaya Hospital in Nicaragua. Vera Clemente said, "A lot of people from [Puerto Rico] went to that inauguration … The hospital was decorated, it had air conditioning, color TV, very pretty, pediatric, it was for children."

Just weeks after the crash, the Baseball Hall of Fame decided to make an exception to its rules in honor of Roberto Clemente. Only the best players are elected to the Hall of Fame. To be considered for election, a player usually has to wait at least five years after appearing in his last game. The rule had only been waived once before, when New York Yankee Lou Gehrig was admitted to the Hall after he **retired** from baseball in 1939. In that case, Gehrig was very sick with the disease that came to bear his name—amyotrophic lateral sclerosis (ALS), popularly known as Lou Gehrig's disease—and would soon pass away, and the Hall wanted to recognize him before his death. The board of directors for the Hall of Fame decided that Roberto Clemente's case deserved a similar exception. On March 20, 1973, just a few short months after his tragic death, Roberto Clemente was elected into the Baseball Hall of Fame. He was officially inducted on August 6, the first Latino player to be selected for baseball's most prestigious honor.

Considering Clemente's experiences with people misunderstanding his Latino heritage, it was particularly ironic that the Hall of Fame originally (and incorrectly) inscribed the name Roberto Walker Clemente on the plaque commemorating his career. Roberto's wife, Vera, noticed the mistake when she later visited the Hall and requested that it be changed. The Hall of Fame corrected the error and produced a new plaque with the correct name, Roberto Clemente Walker.

Roberto Clemente played major league baseball for eighteen years. Among his many accomplishments, he finished with exactly 3,000 hits, a lifetime batting average of .317, two World Series titles, four batting titles, and twelve Gold Gloves.

GAME-CHANGING CHRONOLOGY

August 18, 1934: Roberto Clemente is born in Carolina, Puerto Rico.

1942: Plays on his first organized team, which was in a slow-pitch softball league.

1948: Joins a more competitive little league softball team.

1950: Switches from softball to baseball.

1951-1952: Stars in baseball and track in high school

1952: Signs first professional baseball contract with the Santurce Cangrejeros (Crabbers) of the Puerto Rican Winter League.

1954: Signs first major league baseball contract with the Brooklyn Dodgers; drafted away from the Dodgers by the Pittsburgh Pirates.

1955: Plays his first Major League Baseball game with the Pittsburgh Pirates.

1956: Hits over .300 in the major leagues for the first time.

1958: Leads National League outfielders in assists (22) for the first time; begins six months of service in the United States Marine Corps.

1960: Pirates defeat the New York Yankees in the World Series.

1961: Chosen as the starting right fielder for the National League in the All Star Game; wins his first of twelve Gold Glove Awards; wins his first National League batting title; becomes the first Puerto Rican ever to lead the league in batting average.

1964: Wins second National League batting title; marries Vera Zabala.

1965: Wins third National League batting title.

1966: Gets two thousandth major league hit; wins the National League Most Valuable Player (MVP) award and is named the National League Player of the Year.

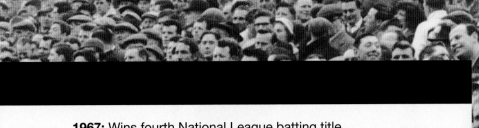

1967: Wins fourth National League batting title.

1970: Roberto Clemente Night is celebrated in Pittsburgh at the Pirates' new home, Three Rivers Stadium.

1971: Pirates win the World Series against the Baltimore Orioles, and Clemente is voted the Most Valuable Player of the Series; attains national stardom.

1972: Gets three thousandth and final regular season hit; becomes the player with most games in a Pirate uniform; wins twelfth and final Gold Glove Award; perishes in a plane crash on New Year's Eve while trying to deliver relief supplies to Nicaragua after a major earthquake.

1973: Elected after his death to the Major League Baseball Hall of Fame; the Pittsburgh Pirates retire Roberto Clemente's number 21; awarded the first **posthumous** Presidential Citizens medal, the second-highest civilian award in the United States.

1974: The Roberto Clemente Sports City is created.

1984: The US Post Office unveils a Roberto Clemente stamp on the fiftieth anniversary of his birth.

1994: A statue of Clemente is erected at Three Rivers Stadium

2002: Major League Baseball announces and celebrates the first Roberto Clemente Day on September 18.

2003: Awarded the Presidential Medal of Freedom by President George W. Bush.

2004: Voted top player in Pirates history.

2006: Awarded the Commissioner's Historic Achievement Award during the All-Star Game in Pittsburgh.

A bronze statue of Hall of Fame right fielder Roberto Clemente stands outside of the home field of the Pirates, PNC Park.

CHAPTER 5

CLEMENTE LIVES ON

"If you have to die, how better could your death be exemplified than by being on a mission of mercy. It was so typical of the man."

—John Galbreath, owner of the Pittsburgh Pirates

Roberto Clemente left the world in the prime of his life. He left behind a loving wife, three young children, countless admirers, and a wealth of memories. He realized many of his dreams but left so many others unfulfilled. If the plane crash of December 31, 1972 had never happened, Roberto Clemente would have turned eighty-one years old in 2015. He had already accomplished so much in the thirty-eight years since his birth. What would he have done with another forty or more years, a greater number of years than he had already lived?

As an athlete, Roberto Clemente was looking forward to returning for his nineteenth season when the accident ended his life. Even though he was thirty-eight years old and had been rested for more games than usual in 1972, he was still an elite hitter and fielder. At an age where many other players retire and begin to plan their life's path after baseball, Clemente was preparing to continue his career. How many more hits would he have gotten? How many more accolades would he have collected? Would he have built on his experience mentoring young Latino players and become a coach? Would he have eventually managed the Pirates, or another big-league team?

And what of his life outside of baseball? How many more children would he have helped? How much more aid would he have delivered to countries in need? Would he have taken charge of an organization to serve even more people on a global scale? Would he have capitalized on his massive popularity and entered politics, perhaps becoming a leader in his native Puerto Rico?

Unfortunately, that plane crash on New Year's Eve, 1972 extinguished the shining light known as Roberto Clemente. We'll never know what he would have achieved. All we can do is wonder what may have been, and consider the complex legacy that Roberto Clemente left behind.

One Life, Many Sides

Roberto Clemente was a complicated man. Some saw only the star baseball player, driven to excel, proud and defiant, angry yet determined. Others knew his other side, the sensitive family man, someone who reached out to those in need, who helped other Latino players adjust to life in the United States and the major leagues, who cared more about others than himself. In truth, Roberto Clemente was both of those men. Shortly after his death, his family, his friends, his teammates, and reporters all tried to express their feelings about what kind of man he was, and how he left his mark on everyone who ever met him.

To some, Clemente appeared to be a mass of contradictions. He could be quick to anger. He was prone to public displays of dissatisfaction, vehemently disagreeing with his managers, umpires, and the writers and announcers who covered the team, when he felt it was necessary. However, those same people could also easily recount how kind and generous Clemente was. Many people thought he was one of the nicest people they ever met. In his book *Clemente: The Passion and Grace of Baseball's Last Hero,* author David Maraniss described Clemente as "shy, yet bursting with pride. He was profoundly humble, yet felt misunderstood and undervalued."

Many who knew him described him as someone who wanted everything to be perfect. He expected great things from everyone, but from himself most of all. He was consumed by the need to "tell it like it is," to speak openly and honestly about anything that concerned him. But people also saw another side of his personality. In his book *Roberto Clemente: Baseball Star and Humanitarian*, author Lew Freedman quotes Luis Mayoral, a long-time friend, as saying, "There was a peaceful Roberto Clemente, a funny Roberto Clemente." His wife Vera remembers that, in addition to being a great father and husband, Roberto liked to write poetry. In the family book about Clemente, his son Luis says that he believed his father "did not trust people easily. But he was very loyal. His old teammates always say, 'Your dad was the best friend and teammate anyone could have.'"

Thirty years after he died in a plane crash, Roberto Clemente was remembered in an exhibit of memorabilia in the Museum of Puerto Rican Art in San Juan, Puerto Rico.

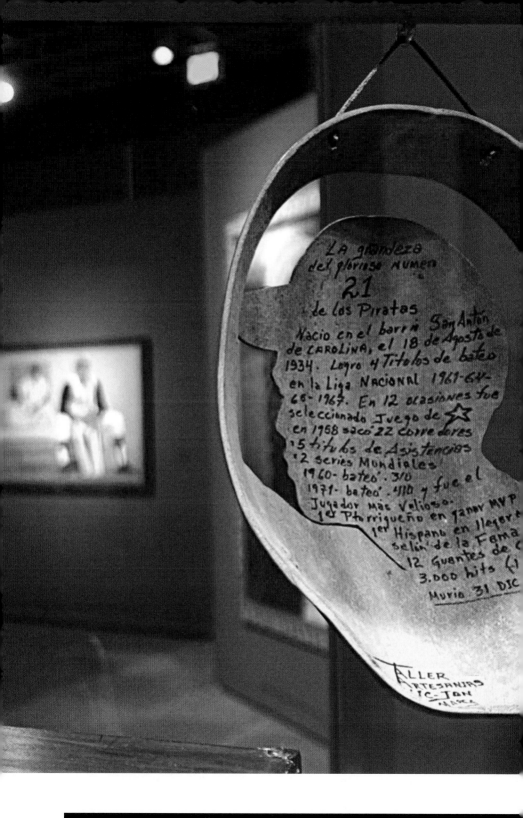

NURTURING ALL LATINOS

Most successful people credit a mentor, an experienced and trusted advisor, for helping them on the road to success. Roberto Clemente gratefully acknowledged the influence and guidance of several people who helped him succeed in baseball, including Roberto Marin, Buzz Clarkson, and Harry Walker. It's difficult, however, to pick one person who credits Roberto Clemente as being *their* mentor, someone whom *they* went to for advice and who taught *them* how to be successful. It's not that such people are hard to find. Quite the contrary. There are too many to count. No list could be comprehensive or broad enough to fully measure the impact that Roberto Clemente had on so many lives.

Clemente helped Matty Alou to become a great hitter, so great that Alou later won the National League batting title. He became a close friend and advisor to Manny Mota, an outfielder with the Pirates and later a coach with the Dodgers who came from the Dominican Republic. Clemente befriended Manny Sanguillen, a catcher from Panama who admired Clemente as he was growing up.

Author Lew Freedman wrote that, according to a 2002 article in the *Orlando Sentinel*, Mota described Clemente as a man who was recognized for his role in standing up for Latino players during an era when dark skin and speaking with an accent often made someone a target for prejudice. "He was a great person, a good human being, a person who would defend minorities," Mota said. "He was a leader and controversial because he did not permit injustices in regards to race. He was vocal, and that was very difficult. He was very misunderstood. But he would not accept injustices with Latinos or with players of color. He was always there to defend them."

In the same article, then Chicago White Sox manager Ozzie Guillen, the first Hispanic manager to win a World Series, said Clemente was an important figure in the history of baseball for more than his on-field accomplishments. "For me, he was the Jackie Robinson of Latin baseball," said Guillen, who is from Venezuela. "He lived racism. He was a man who was happy to be not only Puerto Rican, but Latin American. He let people know that. And that is something that is important for all of us."

Author Jerry Roberts quotes Al Oliver, a Pirates teammate who would eventually garner 2,743 hits of his own over eighteen years in the major leagues: "Outside of my parents, Roberto had the biggest impact on me. He might have been the only one in the organization who understood me. He was raised the same way. He proved you could have an ego and not be egotistical, confident but not cocky, humble when [he] needed to be, but, most of all, maintaining your dignity and self-respect in spite of all the negative obstacles that were in his way."

Tony Taylor, a Cuban second-baseman for the Philadelphia Phillies, told author David Maraniss that he and other Latin American players would go out to eat with Clemente whenever they were in the same city. "He'd try to help you and talk to you about the way to play baseball and the way to handle yourself in society and represent your country," Taylor recalled. "In my life, besides my mom and father, I'd met no person who meant so much to me."

Baseball Remembers

The Pittsburgh Pirates opened the 1973 season with heavy hearts. The players wore Clemente's number 21 on the left sleeve of their uniforms to honor their fallen teammate. The team also forever retired the number, meaning that no other Pittsburgh player will ever wear it.

A statue of Clemente, following through on his swing and beginning his dash to first base, now stands outside the Pirates' stadium. It was originally placed outside Three Rivers Stadium in 1994 during the All-Star Game, and most of the money used to create the statue came from Pirates players. One of them was Orlando Merced, who grew up across the street from Clemente's family in Puerto Rico. Merced told *Sports Illustrated* that "Roberto Clemente means a dream to me, and to a lot of kids and people. I never met him, but I played baseball inside his house, around the Gold Gloves, the silver bats, the trophies, the pictures. He pushed me to be a better ballplayer and a better person. When they unveiled the statue, I was crying. It made me proud to be who I am and to be a Puerto Rican." Clemente's statue was moved to the current Pirates baseball stadium, PNC Park, when their new home opened in 2001. Out in right field, his position, the fence stands exactly 21 feet (6.4 m) high in his honor.

On July 13, 2006, the Pirates hosted the Major League All-Star Game at PNC Park. During the game, the players from both the National and American Leagues wore gold wristbands showing the letters RCW, the initials of Roberto Clemente Walker. That night, Vera Clemente accepted the baseball Commissioner's Historic Achievement Award in Roberto's honor.

Each year, Major League Baseball gives the Roberto Clemente Award to the player who does the most to help others in his community. Baseball created the award in 1971, but after Clemente's death, baseball owners renamed the award to honor a man who lived and died in that spirit.

Creating a Path for Latinos

Roberto Clemente was one of the first Latino players to join a major league roster after Jackie Robinson broke the color line in baseball. His performance helped open the door for other Latinos to play professional baseball in the United States.

Clemente was more than just a great ballplayer to the younger Latino players who came after him. He was a friend and, in many ways, acted like a big brother to Latin American players, especially those who were new to the United States. Roberto remembered how hard it was to adjust to life in America and how lonely he felt. He went out of his way to make life easier for the new Latino players and their families. Clemente helped them to learn English and to find a place to live. He helped them to fit in. Latino players would come to his house for dinner.

In his book on Roberto Clemente's life, author Jerry Roberts quoted his subject as saying that everything was strange to a Latino player who was new to the United States: "The language barrier is great at first. We have trouble ordering food in restaurants. You have no idea how segregation held some of us back … We need time to settle down emotionally. Once we're relaxed and have no problems, we can play baseball well. The people who never run into these problems don't have any idea at all what kind of an ordeal it is."

"I don't care if they're Puerto Rican or not," Clemente told his **chiropractor**, Arturo Garcia. "They can be Dominican, Venezuelan, Cuban, Mexican—they're Latinos, my people."

Today, more than one quarter of all major league baseball players are Latinos. In the minor leagues the percentage is even higher, nearly four out of ten. Roberto Clemente bravely blazed a trail that opened the eyes, and minds, of baseball.

Roberto's Family Carries On

The Clemente family has done its best to carry on a husband's and father's legacy. Roberto's three sons were very young when their father died. Roberto Jr. was seven, Luis was six, and Ricky was three the night of the accident. Long-time family friend Chuck Berry said, "They were never able to have that close relationship with their father because of the accident. They were left with the job of trying to live up to his legend." Youngest son Ricky said, "I was too young to truly get to know my dad, but I've learned everything about him. I try to treat people the way he treated people."

In the Clemente family's book, the boys credit their mother for helping them cope after their father's death. Son Roberto Jr. says, "The best thing my father did was pick a perfect wife and perfect mom for his kids." Brother Luis says of his mother, "She rescued the family. She kept us together. She's a strong woman."

"She still mourns him," says Roberto. "In essence, she is still married to my father." Vera Clemente never remarried. She and her sons continue to pursue the vision her husband started.

Clemente always had an interest in helping young people. David Maraniss wrote that, during his travels with the Pirates in the United States, Clemente had developed a routine of visiting sick children in National League cities. The hospital visits were rarely publicized, but ailing kids everywhere seemed able to find out about them. Before each road trip, he sorted his large pile of mail in the clubhouse and made a special stack for letters from children in cities where the Pirates were headed next.

After the 1964 season, he started something that he had always dreamed of doing. He organized and managed several baseball clinics in Puerto Rico to serve underprivileged children. Clemente credited sports in general, and baseball in particular, for making a tremendous difference in his life, and he wanted to give children in his homeland that same opportunity. Roberto hoped to eventually build a sports complex that could serve all the children of Puerto Rico.

One of Clemente's managers on the Pirates, Danny Murtaugh, said that Clemente's dream of building a sports center for children was typical of how he always thought of things more important than baseball. Murtaugh told writer Jim O'Brien that when Clemente was getting close to getting his three thousandth hit, "I asked him if that would be the most important thing in his life. 'No, Danny,' he said. 'I have a project going in Puerto Rico for the underprivileged.'" He was talking about his plans for a "Sports City" for youth in his homeland.

After the 1971 World Series made him a famous star, he became even more determined to pursue his dream of building a sports city for children in Puerto Rico. Writer Murray Chass wrote an article for the *New York Times* about Clemente's dream in October 1971, in which he said Clemente called the project "the biggest ambition of my life." Clemente told Chass that, "I get kids together and talk about the importance of sports, the importance of being a good citizen, the importance of respecting their mother and father. Then we go to the ball field, and I show them some techniques of playing baseball."

After the plane crash, Vera led an effort to build the Roberto Clemente Sports City in his honor. The island of Puerto Rico donated the land for the center, and many people donated money to make sure that the center was built. Over the next thirty years, thousands upon thousands of children took part in the programs. Some of those children later rose to be Major League

Baseball stars, including Bernie Williams, Juan Gonzales, and Ivan Rodriquez. St. Louis Cardinals catcher Yadier Molina, himself a Puerto Rican, took up the cause of abused and disadvantaged kids through his foundation. Molina says the chance to live up to Clemente's legacy was a motivating factor.

A Man Remembered

Roberto Clemente died more than more than forty years ago, but his name lives on all over the world. Schools, streets, bridges, buildings, and ball fields, all bearing his name, dot the landscape in cities and towns all across the United States. There's a ballpark named for him in Mannheim, Germany, and an award in Japan that honors the Japanese ballplayer who contributes to community service, just as the Roberto Clemente Award honors a major league player in the United States. There are Roberto Clemente scholarships presented through Major League Baseball.

The United States Postal Service honored Roberto Clemente Walker by issuing a postage stamp in his memory—twice. The first appeared August 17, 1984. He was chosen again in 2000, for the Legends of Baseball series. When the first stamp was released, the ceremony included something that he once said: "Accomplishment is something you cannot buy. If you have a chance to do something for somebody, and do not make the most of it, you are wasting your time on Earth."

In 1973, President Richard Nixon signed legislation awarding Roberto Clemente a posthumous Congressional Gold Medal. One of the sponsors of the legislation was Wilmer Mizell, a congressman from North Carolina. Mizell pitched in the major leagues and played alongside Clemente on the Pirates' 1960 World Series championship team. Remembering Clemente, Mizell said, "His power hitting, his blazing base running, his amazing ability as a fielder—all of these are testimony to the fact that he was a complete athlete and a genuine superstar in the game of baseball. This is Roberto Clemente the ballplayer. But the greatest testimonial to how great Roberto Clemente the man was, was the tremendous interest he took in the youth of Puerto Rico."

In July 2003, President George W. Bush awarded Clemente the Presidential Medal of Freedom, the highest honor that a citizen of the United States can receive. Vera Clemente accepted the award on behalf of her late husband.

New York Daily News sportswriter Dick Young once said, "Maybe some guys hit the ball farther, and some throw it harder, and one or two run faster, but nobody puts it all together like Roberto." Roberto Clemente indeed put it all together, in baseball and in life.

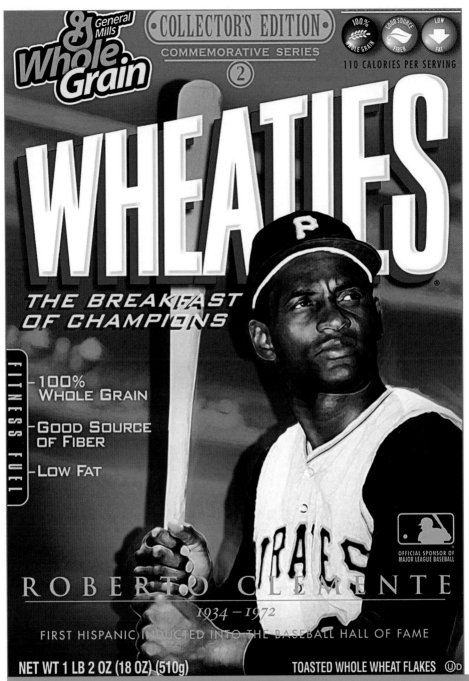

Many famous athletes have graced the cover of a Wheaties cereal box. In 2005, Wheaties celebrated Hispanic Heritage Month with a new special-edition package honoring baseball hall of famer Roberto Clemente.

GLOSSARY

All-Star Game An exhibition game (does not count in the season records) played once a year at midseason between baseball's best players from the American and National Leagues.

amateur A player or athlete who does not get paid.

American League One of the two leagues in Major League Baseball. It is the younger of the two leagues.

assist When a baseball fielder throws a ball to a teammate, who tags a runner or a base to get an out.

batting average The number of hits that a player has had divided by the total number of times he had at bat, shown in three decimal places.

bonus A one-time payment made to a player, usually a prospect, when he signs with a club. It is not part of regular salary.

ceded Surrendered or forced to give up.

chiropractor A health care professional who specializes in treating the back, spine, and nervous system.

color barrier The refusal of major league baseball to allow persons of color to compete on or against teams with white players.

contract A legal agreement between a team and a player that defines terms of employment and payments.

double A hit in baseball on which the batter reached second base without the benefit of an error.

doubleheader Two games in one day.

draft A process by which teams select new players, usually with the teams picking in reverse order of their position in the standings.

error A misplay charged to a fielder who fails to properly catch or throw a ball, resulting in a runner being safe or advancing an extra base.

free agent Someone who has no contract and can sign with any team.

Hall of Fame A museum located in Cooperstown, New York, that highlights the history of baseball.

hit When a baseball player reaches base by hitting the ball and the fielder does not make an error.

home run A hit in baseball on which the batter runs around the bases and scores a run on his or her own hit. It usually occurs when the batted ball lands beyond the outfield fence.

Latino A person who was born or lives in Latin America, countries in the Americas where Spanish or Portuguese are the primary languages.

line drive A hard-hit baseball that travels in a nearly straight line, usually not far above the ground.

GLOSSARY

malaria A serious disease borne by mosquitos, marked by fever and chills, that can cause death.

major leagues The highest level of professional baseball in the United States, comprised of the National and American Leagues.

minor league A lower-level professional league in which athletes with less experience or skill try to prepare for the major leagues.

Most Valuable Player (MVP) A title awarded to a sports player who contributes the most to his or her team's success.

National League The older of the two leagues that make up Major League Baseball in the United States.

Negro Leagues Divisions for professional African-American players who were not allowed to play with whites on Major and Minor League teams. The last of these leagues, the Negro American League, ceased operations in 1960.

pennant The championship for each baseball major league.

playoffs A series of baseball games to decide which teams will play in the World Series.

posthumous After the person's death.

prejudice Unfair treatment that results from holding fixed opinions about a group of people according to their race, religion, gender, or sexual orientation.

professional Someone who is paid for their work or for playing sports.

prospect A young athlete likely to succeed.

quota A limited or fixed amount of people or objects allowed in a group or on a team.

racism Unfair treatment of people based on their race.

retired A player is retired when he or she stops playing; a number is retired when a team decides to no longer use it in honor of someone who wore it.

rookie A player who has taken part in less than a minimum number of games; the player is usually in his or her first season.

runs batted in (RBIs) A baseball statistic that counts the number of runners who score without the benefit of an error when a batter hits the ball.

scouts People who look for new baseball players for a team.

segregated When people of different races are separated in housing, employment, education, or use of public facilities.

triple A hit in baseball on which the batter reaches third base without the benefit of an error.

Winter League A professional baseball league in Puerto Rico that plays during the winter months when the Major Leagues are off.

SELECTED BIBLIOGRAPHY

Books

Clemente Family, The. *Clemente: The True Legacy of an Undying Hero*. New York, NY: Celebra, 2013

Ford, Carin T. *Roberto Clemente: Baseball Legend*. Berkeley Heights, NJ: Enslow Publishers, Inc., 2005

Franchino, Vicky. *Roberto Clemente*. Ann Arbor, MI: Cherry Lake Publishing, 2008

Guzmán, Lila, and Rick Guzmán. *Roberto Clemente: Baseball Hero*. Berkeley Heights, NJ: Enslow Publishers, Inc., 2006

Healy, Nick. *Roberto Clemente: Baseball Legend*. Mankato, MN: Capstone Press, 2006

Maraniss, David. *Clemente: The Passion and Grace of Baseball's Last Hero*. New York, NY: Simon & Schuster, 2006

Musick, Phil. *Who Was Roberto? A Biography of Roberto Clemente*. Garden City, NY: Doubleday Company, 1974

Roberts, Jerry. *Roberto Clemente: Baseball Player*. New York, NY: Ferguson, 2006

Online Articles

Karan, Tim. "21 Facts You May Not Know About Roberto Clemente on the Anniversary of His Debut." *Bleacher Report*. April 17, 2012. http://bleacherreport.com/articles/1149087-21-facts-you-may-not-know-about-

roberto-clemente-on-the-anniversary-of-his-debut.

Markusen, Bruce. "Cooperstown Confidential: MLK and MLB in 1968." *Hardball Times.* February 15, 2013. http://www.hardballtimes.com/cooperstown-confidential-martin-luther-king-and-mlb-in-1968.

Newhan, Ross. "Clemente's Legacy is Told in Human Terms." *Los Angeles Times.* June 3, 2003. http://articles.latimes.com/2003/jun/03/sports/sp-newhan3.

Ortiz, Jorge L. "Clemente's Impact Wanes in Puerto Rico 40 Years After His Death." *USA Today.* December 31, 2012. http://www.usatoday.com/story/sports/mlb/2012/12/27/roberto-clemente-40th-anniversary-death-plane-crash-puerto-rico-pirates-humanitarian/1794453.

PBS. "Introduction: Roberto Clemente." *PBS.* http://www.pbs.org/wgbh/americanexperience/features/introduction/clemente-introduction.

Puga, Kristina. "Roberto Clemente's Family Writes Very Personal Book About a Great Legend." *NBCLATINO.* September 24, 2013. http://nbclatino.com/2013/09/24/roberto-clementes-family-writes-very-personal-book-about-a-great-legend.

FURTHER INFORMATION

Books

Freedman, Lew. *Roberto Clemente: Baseball Star and Humanitarian*. Edina, MN: ABDO Publishing Company, 2011

Markusen, Bruce. *Roberto Clemente: The Great One*. New York, NY: Sports Publishing, 2013.

———. *The Team That Changed Baseball: Roberto Clemente and the 1971 Pittsburgh Pirates*. Yardley, PA: Westholme Publishing, 2009.

Thornley, Stu. *Roberto Clemente*. Minneapolis, MN: Twenty-First Century Books, 2007

Virtue, John. *South of the Color Barrier: How Jorge Pasquel and the Mexican League Pushed Baseball Toward Integration*. Jefferson, NC: McFarland, 2007.

Videos

The Legacy of Roberto Clemente
m.mlb.com/video/topic/7417714/v63856383/mlb-now-looks-at-the-legacy-of-roberto-clemente/?query=Roberto%2BClemente
A video produced by the MLB network about the life and legacy of Roberto Clemente.

Roberto Clemente – Baseball Hall of Fame Biographies

baseballhall.org/hof/clemente-roberto

This short film from the Hall of Fame in Cooperstown showcases some of the great skills of this marvelous player while providing a narrative of his career and his death.

Roberto Clemente: More Than Baseball

www.schooltube.com/video/bc56c787c099351c3e9d/
Roberto-Clemente-More-Than-Baseball_

This five-minute video contains scenes and narration that cover Roberto Clemente's career.

Roberto Clemente's 3,000th Hit

www.youtube.com/watch?v=XsmqqPxb_xM

Watch the legendary right fielder double for his final hit in the major leagues.

Organizations

Baseball Hall of Fame

baseballhall.org

Pittsburgh Pirates

pittsburgh.pirates.mlb.com/pit/history/pit_clemente.jsp

Smithsonian Institution

www.robertoclemente.si.edu/english/index.htm_

INDEX

Page numbers in **boldface** are illustrations. Entries in **boldface** are glossary terms.

Gerry Boehme was born in New York City, graduated from The Newhouse School at Syracuse University, and now lives on Long Island with his wife and two children. His many interests include being a published author and editor, a businessperson, and a guest speaker at conferences across the United States as well as the United Kingdom, Australia, and the Republic of Korea.